# Music

## *And the Art of Being Human*

# Phil Goddard

**Musings on Love**

Published by The Happy Discovery -
www.thehappydiscovery.com

Contact the author - www.philg.com

Cover quote: James Brett

Second Edition  - January 2018

ISBN-10: 1521748993

ISBN-13: 978-1521748992

# For Ben

# Acknowledgments and Gratitude

To Ben, the perfect coach whilst I fumbled along as a parent.

To Steve Chandler, for lessons on coaching and life beyond count.

To Robert Holden, for teaching me so much about love, not least the distinction between love and all else.

To Michael Neill, for your entertaining ways of teaching the principles of the human experience.

To my Mum, for everything that a mum does, and so much more.

To friends who have supported these musings, loved me and encouraged me in the creation of this book.

To all of my clients, for the joy of exploring the art of the possible and the human spirit of creation.

To you, yes you reading this, for being the inspiration for this writing.

With love always, thank you!

"The music ain't worth nothing if you can't lay it on the public."
~ Louis Armstrong


To everyone and anyone who has ever liked, commented on, or shared one of my Facebook posts, thank you!

You may paint your face or paint your wheels.

Go lunch with your ego and shade yourself from the shining of truth.

I'm not interested in what your vanity commands, or your worldly opinions sourced from fear and misjudgements.

I want to see what is in your heart, and for what purpose your soul desires you use the rest of your life.

I want to know what would have you cry with joy in your last breath, and glow in immense love for your own life.

I want to know you. Do you?

# Read Me

Many times, people have said to me 'you should write a book.' So here is a gathering of my writings over the last few years. Some of it will feel familiar, perhaps because you have followed me on social media, or because truth is often something we recognise.

There is a common thread that runs through much of these musings and all of my work; how each of us thinks our ways out of love, how love is our essential nature, and that all else is a construct of our process of thought.

It seems, then, that all that we think of as a big deal is created by our thinking. Surely nothing can be a big deal without us thinking it so.

Except love. For it is love that is the energy of creation. It is love that keeps you alive as the trillions and gazillions of cells in your body, and in every living thing, only serve to keep us alive.

It must be, then, that the only big deal is love.

Herein are my musings on love.

# Story of My Life

Here's the story of my life:

Born. Life is incredibly simple. Feel happy.

Grow up. Learn to be an 'adult' and learn to make life incredibly complex. Forget to feel happy and choose anxious, stressful, angry, disappointed, sad and frustrated instead.

Wake up. Remember that life is incredibly simple. Feel happy.

*No problem can exist in the absence of thought.*

# Who am I?

I'm someone who grew up in the shadow of three elder siblings, and someone who through most of my life had struggled with weight, loneliness and fitting in. I've been subjected to sexual abuse, grew up in an anti-religion family with a father who kept himself distant from his children.

I'm someone who fell into my original career yet became such an incredibly successful leader that people followed me from one organisation to another, and eventually became strong enough to give it all up and stand up for what I believe. I sent the email that said "Things either have to change or we manage my exit" and then managed my exit from that company.

At age 20 I went from having dinner put on the table by my mother to being an overnight stepfather to two children, and then in an abusive marriage that was more like a warzone of emotional and physical trauma and abuse.

I've taken the suicidal overdose and done the emergency trip to hospital.

I've been through a second divorce when I woke up to the fact I didn't love my second wife in the way I wanted to as a husband, and realised I had married into a lifestyle, not a partnership. I've also had the love of my life leave me broken and torn.

I now enjoy the most beautiful, loving, deeply connected relationships. Love truly is in abundance in my life.

My father completely disowned me and refused to speak to me during the most challenging 10 years of my life. Yet my best friend in the world is without question or doubt my own son. We are best of mates, have been since he was 8, and our relationship has been the envy of many fathers I know with teenage kids. He is probably my best coach.

I've been almost broke, having quit my job and invested everything I had into developing as a coach, and even borrowed money to attend Steve Chandler's school. I am willing to lay it all on the line for what I believe.

Some of my favourite coaching success stories are the 19-year-old girl with a beautiful voice, too afraid and shy to sing any place other than her bedroom or even in front of her own parents, and then having worked with me has been auditioning for TV talent shows and singing in public and on stage. I love the story of the guy who turned up suicidal, on antidepressants and who, after exactly 47 minutes, broke out in tears of laughter, freedom and joy, hasn't taken any pills since and has been accused of being on happy-pills by his colleagues.

I'm inspired by the last line of a recent testimonial from a client who, when we started working together, didn't enjoy life, felt intimidated, dark, out of place, yet that line said "I now find there are so many exciting and wonderful things to discover in the World I hardly know where to begin."

I coach from a place of pure uncontaminated love, often very gentle and graceful, yet I am always willing to bring out the proverbial wet mackerel and ask "So fucking what?"

I work with people who are willing to connect deeply with themselves and their capacity to be in love with life. In doing so they create a life of effortless passion guided by true inner wisdom.

I coach deeply guided by my intuition. It is often challenging, and we may go to places within you that you did not know existed. My intention is for you to know you, and to fully be you.

There are no rules, no scripts, no prerequisites or techniques.

We explore. We dance. We create. You thrive.

I bring ALL of me into the coaching relationship and I have learned that the more of me I bring, the more there is for people to connect with.

Yes, I am unique. Just like everyone else.

# Ready is a Mirage

I speak to a lot of people that are not ready. Very few of us ever are. It can take some people an inordinate amount of time to 'get ready', a realization I've had many times whilst living with a partner.

Ready is just a state of mind upon which we'll often put external dependencies. I won't allow myself to FEEL ready until these circumstances are met. I can't go out without make up, I have to have x amount of savings before I buy this widget, or I won't go to the dinner party until I've lost ten pounds.

All conditions for feeling ready are made up. Fabricated! That feeling of being ready is something we create once we see those conditions being met, yet that feeling is available any time.

Ready is a self-made mirage, one for which we need not wait. There might be a moment when the mirage looks real enough for us to step forward, or we might just be waiting forever. The weight and burden of forever as ready becomes a self-obsessive distraction from taking action.

There is an alternative: Willingness. I can ask myself "Am I willing?" Irrespective of how I feel about being ready. Irrespective of the mirage.

Just be willing. Willing to jump out of the plane, willing to pick up the phone, willing to try the deep-fried squid. Willing to ask the question I want an answer to at the conference.

At aged twenty there was no way I was ready to become an overnight step-parent. But I was willing. Looking back, I don't think I was ready until a good few years later!

Some people tell me they are not ready for coaching. Often, they are not willing to see the truth about not being ready. Not willing to do what might be necessary to make such an investment in themselves. Not willing to explore and take the next required action to create the life they want.

As a coach, I always want to explore this, because I'll happily work with many people that are not ready. But I don't work with anyone who is not willing.

It's a simple distinction between wanting some assurance on what an outcome might be, or being willing to explore what we might create and uncover.

If I'm in the 'need to be ready' camp I'm kind of open to corruption, similar to the researcher who is sponsored by an organization with an invested interest in the results. As an independent explorer, I have no such contamination, I am free and open to all possibilities. I don't need to see an imagined mirage of what the road ahead might look like. I am willing, in my faith, to explore and see what shows up.

Blind faith? Yes, of course, all faith is blind.

An entering into that which is not yet seen or not yet known. Entering into that which may soon be seen and known.

I wonder if anyone who has sky-dived actually felt ready as their legs hung over the ledge of the airplane. Or whether, in that moment, it was simply a case of being willing to jump, to fall, to surrender to gravity and the saviour of a parachute. It's not something I have experienced because I am definitely not WILLING to jump out of a perfectly serviceable aircraft.

I'd guess no child waits to be ready before they attempt to take their first steps on their feet. They simply explore, willing to give it a go, time and time again, even after falling down. Again. After a fall, they don't tell themselves "Right, that's it! Clearly, I'm not ready, I'll try again in a couple of years!" They are willing to explore in the direction of their desire (the shiny keys on the table,) irrespective of the outcome (a grazed knee.)

They are not waiting for the mirage of walking to appear clear enough. A grazed knee is nothing to the joys of walking, running, hopping, skipping and jumping for the next eighty years!

Be willing.

# The Illusion of Stability

How often do we strive for some kind of stability in life?

I'll bet the top two desires of stability are a stable relationship and a stable job or income.

Whenever I'm focusing on either creating or finding stability I'm limiting my experience of life, much like stabilisers on a push bike limit the experience of the ride.

Life has so much more to offer than restrictive stability. Who wants to dance with their feet tied together?

Our quest for stability is always ultimately futile, since nothing can be either retained or preserved.

That futile quest always takes us out of the current moment, this one, the only one we ever have, in which the universe is presenting itself to us in all its present splendour. This beautiful moment that we miss because of our obsession with insuring against a future one.

We're all going to die. Our relationships will change shape.

Spending our energy on resisting that and imagining we can do something about it takes us out of the present moment. Chasing the illusion of stability effectively kills us before we die.

Embracing it and realising we are always okay with it liberates us, and frees us from the shackles of insecurity.

Only then may we dance without hindrance and in alignment with nature itself. To me, at least, that looks like the most joyous way to truly live whilst we're alive.

All things are in a state of flux. All stability is imagined.

*Home isn't where the heart is.*
*Home is what the hearts is.*

# Creating my story

Today I will create a story

It will be the story of my life. Everything I imagine to be real will be real. Everything I wish to be I will be. Everything I choose not to be I will not be.

I have been doing this every single day of my entire life.

*I thought I was happy. And so I was.*

# Stop Searching

There is so much more power in allowing than seeking. We can only ever seek wearing blinkers of our conditioning, looking for the answers we think will solve our problems and questions. "Seek and ye shall find." Yet by seeking and searching we only ever find what we are looking for. We miss the infinite possibilities for which we are not searching.

So many of us spend our lives searching, blinkered and almost blind, in a bind, caught up in a nightmare of not having the answers we think we need.

What if we switch from searching to allowing? Allowing ourselves to not know and allow any answers to come to us. We don't need to go to them; how can we? We rarely know where they hang out.

Allowing has the full power of the universe behind it. When we are open to all possibilities we are presented with the extraordinary miracles of the universe. When we embrace, and embody all possibilities through our openness we realise our powerful flow as part of the universe.

If we feel we need answers we do not need to search for them. They are presented to us when we clear the way for them. Any reason is not our reasoning. The wisdom of the universe has no opinion or investment in your being. It just is.

# Faking It Until You Make It

You don't need to 'Fake' anything to make it.

You can, of course, pretend to be something you are not, and yes, after a while you'll find you will have built this habit of being that person you wanted to be. Yet, all the time you are pretending you will not be being, and therefore expressing, your true self. Whilst you 'fake it' you are effectively lying to yourself until you decide to believe yourself, and in that process the same can be said of how others will see you.

Once you realise that you are the creator of all in your life, your whole experience of life, and by realise I literally mean real-ise, make it real, you can move beyond the notion that you need to pretend anything. You can move to the realisation that you can BE the one that proclaims and embodies the I AM THAT.

As the only creator of who you are in any moment, through your own beliefs about you which you choose to be true, you get to choose you.

You don't need to pretend anything. Why pretend when you can create?

Create you.

# We Are All Going to Die

I'll give you any odds you want on anyone reading this being alive in 100 years' time.

We all know it, even if at times we don't want to believe it. A dear friend and coaching mentor of mine stood on stage at an event I was at last year and told us "We're all going to die, and we don't know when."

This is perhaps our ONLY truth.

With this knowing there are many things in life that we simply allow not to affect us in any way. We'll 'be gone long before then' or we 'have more important things to worry about.'

Yet so often we lose sight of that perspective. We are going to die.

February the 10th this year will be my 17,000th day alive, according to a nice little app on my phone. Wow, where did they all go? Well, I can tell you that a whole bunch of them went on being concerned about things that even at day 17,000, let alone my last day, will be of no concern to me whatsoever!

A few times I've been asked 'if this were your last day what would you do' or a variation of that question, such as 'if you only had one year to live what would you do?' The last time that latter question was asked I simply considered, well, I'd probably spend more time hanging out and having a good few beers with my mates. Oh, gosh, what does that mean? That I don't want my life to mean anything? That I don't want to leave some kind of legacy? Well, Maybe...

I'm okay with dying. I was talking to my mother just this weekend about this. Seriously, if I go now, tonight or next weekend, I'm pretty much okay with it. Sure, there are things I would love to do, but there will always be, and I am at peace with my own mortality. I'd feel for those close to me (if I could), I know I am important to a few people's lives, but for me personally, I'm okay with my mortality.

Another mentor of mine, Michael Neill, talked about this once, can you be okay with today being a good day to die? Yes... I think I can. I think I am. I am at peace with it. It no longer has to be of concern to me. I am free of the fear.

And whilst I'm here...

I see it all the time. All over Facebook, all over my friends and family's faces, all over their lives. An obsession with life as if it is all that there is. Sure, I get it, we (maybe) just have this one life and we're a long time dead. But I also get that if there are molecularly minuscule details about life that are not 'going my way' I am not going to contaminate this magically brief momentary visit to this realm with beating shit that things are not how I imagined or want them to be.

I choose to live and embrace every moment. I might not enjoy all moments, I'm magnificently human in that I might not even enjoy complete phases of the journey that might feel like an indestructible, era defining feat of apocalyptic architecture of my life, but I also know I'll be gone soon enough, and way before then, so also will be this very moment.

THIS moment.

Gone.

Left behind will be, God's will winning over the arrogance of man, a beautiful planet of natural, blissful harmony in which my own ashes and memories may still be a part.

Whatever I think is a big deal, in all likelihood isn't. It just feels that way when I am blinded by my own illusion of my own life. There is so much more to life than me, than my own often pathetic details, than my own thoughts.

Yes, that's it. There is more to this existence, this being, this relentless alive and beautiful universe than my own transient, momentary and immeasurably small thoughts about my own brief life. And when I allow myself a glimpse of that, when I see that I am not even a conceivable part of the blue dot, I'm at peace, I feel the bliss of insignificance that allows me a playful exploration of the possible, and indeed seemingly impossible, within my own illusionary world.

And I allow my own miracles to unfold. I allow myself to just be me.

# Morning Meanings

Some mornings I wake up almost in tears because of how beautiful my life seems.

Some mornings I wake up almost in tears because of how much of a mess my life seems.

Not much changes between these mornings.

# What if...

What if 'What if' holds you back?

What ifs that hold you back, rather than invite you to step forward.

What if they think I'm stupid? What if they think I'm needy? What if they think I'm not successful?

They tend to focus on what others think, but not always.

What if I fall over? What if I stumble or forget my words?

Even these often have a focus on what others think of us.

Yet ultimately, each 'What if' is really only concerned with what we think of ourselves.

What if I crap my pants before going on stage? People will think... which will mean I am....

I am something other than what I want to believe I am.

These types of 'What ifs' can take people to dangerous places, even suicide, because they keep us disconnected from not just others and the world, but from the love we always have inside our self.

These are the people that retreat to the back of the room when the dance music comes on, or might finally admit they've had a tough time and didn't feel able to ask for help. Sometimes they seem aloof or at best, distant. When we meet them we might feel a sense that there is more to see, that they are maintaining that self-image and hiding behind it.

Cracks always appear.

They need our love. If it's you, you need your love to allow us to also love you.

Let us in.

# Don't Abandon Your Fears

As a six to eight-year-old I suffered some quite traumatic nightmares. My Mum would fetch me out of bed and take me downstairs and sit with me on the sofa, whilst all the time the nightmare would continue. Even though I was no longer actually sleeping I'd have spells of sheer terror, calling out and pointing ahead of me "They're coming now! They're right there!!"

My Mum just sat with me, holding me, doing nothing other than comforting me and being with me.

I learned later that my Dad's view of these episodes was that I should have been put back to bed and left to get on with it. The dreams would pass anyways.

I don't know what might have become of me if my Mum had agreed with him or not stood her ground in refusing to do that, but I sense that these nightmare episodes may have had a greater impact on me. Looking back at them now they are a time of comfort, feeling my Mum loving me and being there with me, and I guess my

Dad's alternative would mean I'd look back on them as times of abandonment.

My Mum seemed to instinctively know she needed to do nothing with my fears, with my nightmares, just be with me and love me, and they would pass.

Something I've since learned to do for others and for myself.

# The Healing Illusion

There really is no process to go through. Your past is not part of you in any way, other than how you have allowed your experiences to condition your thinking.

We can argue that your thinking has an impact on your physical being, that I believe to be true, but only in the same way that what I have eaten has an impact on my physical body too, and by simply changing what I eat now my body will also change. You don't have to go through any process to deal with your past thoughts, just change your relationship with your thinking.

Suggesting that no human is completely free of unhealed pain is a great observation, because pain is indeed part of the human experience and most people do not completely understand the simple thought-feeling connection through which they experience every single moment of life.

Whilst I'm an advocate of not denying pain, indeed not denying anything that has happened in our past, I also believe in the liberation that the realisation of where these experiences comes from can bring.

There is no pain stored in your body in so much as there is no burger and fries from last month's trip to In-n-Out stored in your body. There might be some representation in your body of you experiencing that pain just as there might be of you having had the burger and fries, but you don't need to go through some healing process or ritual to work through it.

"Imagine yourself reversing back into the drive-thru. You hand back the brown paper bag containing the burger and fries. Look into the server's eyes and say 'Thank you, but no thank you.'"

Nopes... not at all necessary.

We ONLY have now. Reinvention is possible in any moment, including this one. And this one. And indeed, this one.

Reinvention is possible without you needing to do anything at all about your past. You do not need to heal your past, only understand it is past. Gone. It is no longer now.

Releasing your hold on the big bag you have been carrying is not any kind of denying or repression. It is liberation and a realisation of the truth of Now.

Putting that bag down doesn't mean it is going to continue to grow underneath. There is no need to even open it all up and shuffle through its contents.

Diseases, suicides, violence and addictions are not a symptom of repressed pain. Pain cannot be repressed. It is either felt or it is not. And it is only felt when we believe our painful thoughts. Those thoughts might be that we think we should not allow the free expression of our pain or any other emotions.

Let's stop making something real that is not. Your painful experiences do not take up residence in your existence and squat within you until you 'deal with them.' All that happens is that we allow our experiences to condition our way of thinking, and sometimes that conditioning creates habitual thinking that is painful.

Our liberation comes, not from some process of relinquishing our past, but understanding where our experience of our past is coming from - our thinking about our past. Our liberation comes from the realisation that we are not our thoughts, we are not obliged to believe any of our thoughts, including any painful thoughts we might habitually have entertained about our past experiences.

If you don't like your current thought, let it pass through. All thoughts do pass through.

Those that proliferate beliefs that healing requires some joyous, magnificent recognition are showmen, illusionists creating an act out of the unreal.

Just put the bag down.

# Escape Freedom

Freedom, unless tasted, is unknown, and only it's knowing reveals the irrelevance of all else, the irrelevance of the dreams and illusions of freedom imagined by the imprisoned mind that believes it must be freed.

More often than not, the quest for freedom becomes a search that distracts from what is already here, and ironically it is the freedom of now that is overlooked.

Only by escaping this quest of the concept of freedom can we truly experience the freedom that is always here. Our liberation comes from our realisation that we are, and have always been, free.

*We only suffer to the extent that we believe what we think.*

# You Don't Suck

Often when something amazing happens or is achieved we'll pile praise such as 'You are ahhhmaaaazzzzing!' Yet reinforcing such positive beliefs has a flip side, that when things don't go so well we think we're not so amazing. The flip side of being amazing looks like we suck.

But 'Yes, that sucks!' is not the same as 'you suck!'

There are a million reasons you are indeed ahhhmaaaazzzing, and just because something didn't quite go to plan doesn't change that.

Nothing outside of you means you are amazing or you suck. Whatever happens in life, you are the same beautiful human spirit that arrived here, albeit one with a little more human experience.

Frankly, some event and some days do look like they totally suck. And that usually means we've forgotten the bigger picture of just how beautiful and amazing it is to be human, here on this planet.

'You suck' is an outright lie.

"Yes, it sucks, and you are just as beautiful and amazing" is a better truth.

# You Are Never Sad

How often do we hear people say something like "I am sad" or "I am anxious"?

Laying some kind of claim of identity to these feelings. Yet, these are just emotions, they are neither who or what we are. We are able to feel them, in that we are the feeler of the emotions, the one who experiences them. And yet, in a sense, even that is not true, since I am able to observe the one who is feeling sad, as well as the one who observes the sadness.

The move from the one who 'is sad' to the one who observes the sadness often looks quite a leap. A door to that is simply to realise that you are not the emotion, and to bring that realisation into how you speak of yourself in the world. The simple change from 'I am sad' to 'I feel sad' liberates you from the identity of sadness. Sure, it moves your identity to the one who feels, but it is in this realm that we are able to embrace and allow ourselves to experience emotions without them having to mean anything about us, without them defining who we are, since we are not the 'I am' in that sadness.

As we observe the feeling of sadness, or indeed any emotion, we can see that there is someone who is feeling it, who is not the observer, since the observer is the one who sees the one who is feeling. Yet more freedom comes from this, since we need not identify even with he who feels anything other than what is there without all thought generated emotions.

We can see the thoughts that incite the emotions, and in that we can observe the thinker that thinks the thoughts that lead to the emotions. And who am I without those thoughts?

Love. I am Love.

# Choose

In everyday language, we see it - 'it made me feel.'

If you changed that one thing to 'I chose to feel' it would change your life.

The language we are using is creating our reality of life. 'It made me feel' is the language of a victim.

Whenever you say 'it made me feel' or 'they made me feel' you are lying to yourself. But only every time.

I recall in March 2003, laying on a sun lounger in Sharm El Sheik, reading Stephen Covey's 'The Seven Habits of Highly Effective People.' In that book, Covey quotes Viktor Frankl – *"Between stimulus and response there is a space. In that space is our power to choose our response. In our response lies our growth and our freedom."*

In this one sentence, I realized we are the ones creating our experience of life. Every feeling I have is a choice. I may as well stop lying to myself about that, at least.  And as I remind myself of what my choices are, I see more choices.  I see I really am free.

# Let Doubt Guide You to Love

Most of us will slow down and often stop when we feel doubt. Yet few of us use doubt as a reminder to reconnect with love.

If I am experiencing doubt I am often listening to fearful thoughts. Simply noticing this helps us to consider an alternative to fear.

Doubt can always be an invitation to slow down, to pause and allow your connection to inner wisdom, the wisdom of love.

One of my favourite questions when feeling doubt or confusion is: What would love do?

Almost everyone who sits in this inquiry finds an answer appears that is clear and has no fear attached.

Unlike searching for answers, allowing ourselves to be with and feel love, reconnects us with a greater intelligence that is always available to us, allowing answers to come into our awareness that guide us with peace and clarity.

If you allow them, answers will always come from love to you, because you yourself are love.

# What to do with Sadness

Throat choking sadness… what to do with it?

In some ways, a strange question. I know when I feel happy the thought "what shall I do with this happiness?" never occurs to me. I know I don't need to do anything with it.

Yet with sadness, and often with anger, anxiety and any other 'uncomfortable' emotion, the question occurs, often unconsciously, what shall I do with this?

In some respects, it's all about expression; expressing anger by shouting, sadness perhaps by crying, anxiety by fidgeting or pacing. So, what do we do with happiness? Often smile, often nothing at all, just being with it. Being with happiness.

When I notice I am happy I don't feel compelled to do something with it in the same way as when I feel anger or sadness. Yet all we need do with any emotion is simply be with it. No emotion actually means we must take action, such as sending that irate email when angry, or dancing in the supermarket aisles when happy, (although I do recommend this way of shopping!)

Being with our emotions is all we ever need do. Accompany them on their journey through us, thanking them for reminding us we are alive and human.

In allowing any emotion to flow, if there is any message to be heard it is easier to hear when we're open and listening, rather than searching or already creating meaning by taking some immediate action.

If I think I need to do something with any emotion I am resisting simply allowing it to be.

And whilst being with that throat choking sadness may bring tears, any message of wisdom will only be heard in the silent space that appears when we stop resisting and allow the feeling of sadness to pass through.

What do you hear when you are not trying to change how you feel?

May any tears you have be the rain that nurtures your heart's desire to love.

# Quit Mustubating!

Whenever we tell ourselves we 'must' do something we are attempting to be alone and separate.

Mustubating is a bad habit that makes you blind.

Blind to other options, opportunities and the infinite possibilities of the universe.

While you're at it, how about you stop shoulding on yourself too?

# The Irrelevance of Fear

If we are aware of the distinction that we have an unconditioned self, the being, the spirit that arrived here, rather than being created here, that spirit being of love. Very quickly, when we arrive here, we become aware that we are a separate self, not immediately I don't imagine, although we cannot know because babies, when first born, seem to not talk about such spiritual matters very much. I imagine it just takes a little while to click "Oh! You're a you, and I'm a Me."

There's an 'I' here, I'm a separate being to you. And in that moment the whole drama of creating a self-image begins...

All of the fears that we have, only really exist within that realm, within that illusion of a self-image and of a separate self.

It is a judgement that we have that death might be a bad thing. But none of us really knows. It's certainly a conditioned thing. I invite you to consider that death being bad is a judgement we make. Indeed, we are able to consider death as a good thing under certain circumstances, such as in cultures where a death penalty is celebrated, or indeed the passing of a loved one after much suffering.

We arrive here, we're a spirit and we're having a human experience, and then we return home. Who's to say that returning home is a bad thing?

If we consider that any fear can be deconstructed to a fear of death, or as A Course in Miracles describes our basic fear - am I loveable, or as I paraphrase that - am I taken care of? - fear in itself can only exist within the realm of a separate self and as a self-image.

Its only your self-image that sees you as a separate self.

If we are open to the possibility that we are always taken care of, even if, gulp, that means we return home, a.k.a. die, if that ultimately means being taken care of, fear only exists within a self-image.

# Divine Intervention

You are the divine that intervenes. You are divine intervention. You are Love.

It is simply for you to consider if your intervention is guided from the divine you have within, or some egoic fantasy of intellect of how you think life should be.

It is for you to choose to listen to your unconditioned self, to listen to the Love that you are, and to intervene, to act with loving kindness.

*People connect deeply to the humanness we so often try to hide.*

# Holding You Back

Nothing but nothing will hold you back as much as this one thing.

Not your supposed limited experience, not your comparative place in your marketplace, not your lack of funds, connections, free time, lack of training or credentials, not your lack of grounding, depth of understanding, lack of energy, lack of a car, your fitness or your health challenges, not your location or education, not your childhood or demands of parenthood, not your attire or lack of a bright red woolly hat for the cold winter's day.

Nothing will hold you back as much as listening to the voice of your self-image.

It is that voice that is providing a commentary on all those supposed reasons why you 'cannot.' Without that voice, all these things are just circumstances, they are just tables and chairs scattered around the dance floor for you to dance around.

But you can't dance whilst sitting at the table of ego scoffing your meal of self-obsession.

There may be ways to deal with each of those circumstances and doing so will, in many cases, help you, but they never need prevent you from dancing, especially if you are willing to bump into the furniture occasionally and even stumble and crash into a table and send the crockery flying.

Nothing, but nothing, holds you back as much as your obsession with your self.

You can love your self-image.  Learn to love the dance more.

# Somebody

Whenever anyone tells you, "You need to be this way..." they are always directing you away from your own wisdom and your true self. Be it in a mastermind, a sisterhood circle, a one-on-one coaching relationship, prescription only ever takes you away from your own inner guidance, wisdom and love.

Whilst often well intended, this kind of advice just has us strive to meet yet another definition of ourselves.

When we define we confine.

The moment someone tells you how to be, they're really telling you how not to be your true self, because any time you try to be somebody you are distracted away from who you truly are; the you that simply shows up when you're not trying to be someone.

Alas, it is a curse of the self-help profession that seems to proliferate this type of unintentional self-obsession. It's really coaching the ego rather than helping you to allow your true self to appear.

Even when you are trying to be yourself you can only ever try to conform with the image you have of yourself, which is entirely fabricated from years of conditioning and beliefs.

It is only when you stop trying to be somebody, stop trying to be anybody, stop trying to even be yourself, that you are truly free. Without any conformity.

The easiest way to allow this is to go do what you love in the word. Contrary to much in the self-help profession, this outward focus of giving your love to what you do will actually allow your inner self to appear, no self-obsession required. Your love for what you do will show the world you.

What's it like to be you when you're not trying to be somebody? What's it like to be you when you're not even trying to be yourself?

# The Next Now

"For a long time, it had seemed to me that life was about to begin - real life. But there was always some obstacle in the way. Something to be got through first, some unfinished business, time still to be served, a debt to be paid. Then life would begin. At last it dawned on me that these obstacles were my life."
~ Fr. Alfred D'Souza (in Obstacles of Life)

Life is a series of nows that we so often fill with events of our past or dreams of our future. We'll live in the now just as soon as we've booked our next holiday, signed our next client, or lost that ten pounds. We so often spend our now looking for the next now, a constant quest for better and more.

And then the next now arrives and the cycle continues. We're never fully present to where we are and to the wonderful experience of life that is always on offer to us, in every moment, right here, right now.

Now is the only time and place you can ever be. And whilst you might be enjoying this now, reading this book, (thank you!) what might life be like if your commitment to the next now was simply to be present to it when it arrived?

And here it is.

Now.

Enjoy.

With love.

*The only reason you're ever unhappy is because you think you should be.*

# The Craze of Meaning

What's with the latest craze that everything has to mean something?

Particularly in a sexual sense, where a woman craves and accepts her man whilst laying claim and owning her own sexuality and her man must comply whilst owning and claiming and seducing and exerting and sharing his deepest cravings... then a vibrating unicorn shows up with the biggest rubber dildo even a well-hung horse has ever seen and claims everyone... except they forgot to claim the lotto....

Seriously, what's with all the meaning?

It's all still playing within a realm of ego and self-image. Masculine this, feminine that. Energies, yes, sure everything is energy, but not identities.

Just express love and love each other.

When the two of you crawl into bed, or lay on the kitchen table in Ikea if that's your thing, and actually talk to each other, get to know each other, communicate in a way that has no judgements and no expectations of you being the one and only unicorn that can lay claim to the orgasmic bliss the mermaid lithes and wishes for herself, without all that noise, you will connect deeply.

Talk. Connect. Lay with each other and explore.

Because whilst some dude on YouTube may claim that all men want a cock worshipping posh whore who will make a sandwich after swallowing, that's just one man's view and opinion and will never, ever ever ever replace the understanding and intimacy of simply listening to, connecting and openly exploring with your partner, without your ego. Simply trusting in love.

# Undefined

Each time you say "It is..." or "I am..." you define and hence confine.  Every definition has edges, constrictions, a denial to our infinite possibilities.

You can't say something 'is' without excluding what it is not.  For any belief you hold you deny whatever may serve you that contradicts that belief.

So much change work centres around your belief system, changing to more positive, empowering beliefs. Yet every single belief you have acts as a definition and hence confinement of who and what you are.

When you see beliefs as the completely optional, constructed thought patterns that they are, when you see they need have no meaning or voting rights on how you live, you are free.

Don't be blinded to infinity by the definition and confinement of beliefs.  Believe only in the infinite.  Be unconfined.  Be undefined.  Be free.

# Know Limits

When I think I know, I am limited to the extent of my knowledge.

When I am willing to be with not knowing, I am open to infinite possibilities, often waiting to be uncovered by lovingly curious exploration.

There are no limits.

Stop knowing.

Start exploring.

# The Enlightened Baby

When I was a baby, I refused to giggle and laugh until I was sure I would have a good job with great prospects, a couple of good holidays a year, a nice house and a big luxury car.

When I was a baby, I decided I was going to be miserable unless people around me behaved in a certain way, and that it was sunny and warm outside, and there was only good news on TV.

Whilst I was a baby, I would only play if I knew I could win, or that the outcome was certain, or I would gain from it in some way.

When I was a baby, I steadfastly refused to be happy unless certain conditions in my life were met. I kept adding to this list of rules for happiness, and each time something on it was met I would add a whole bunch of other rules.

When I was a baby, I decided not to be happy 'unless' or 'until.'

Well... ok... maybe it was a little after I was a baby...

# Only the Ego Thinks It Needs to be Bold

Being bold, just like having confidence, is a red herring! There's a plethora of stories that proliferate the illusion that these are necessary attributes for success, and many of these stories are extremely compelling. Almost every day I see something from a fellow coach or someone in the personal development profession suggesting ways we should and could become bolder, more courageous, more confident.

But you don't need to become more of anything! I suggest the opposite is true, it would serve all of us to become less. Become less concerned with the voice of our own self-image. Become less of a separate being fearful of some egotistic Armageddon in a nightmare that has us rejected and disappear into dust. Yes, we're all going to be dust someday, but what if in the meantime, we focused on being of service from the heart, without allowing interference of BS stories from the ego?

Only the ego believes it needs to be bold or confident, and if allowed this becomes a never-ending quest for yet more. More moreness! More boldness, more confidence, more some-other-made-up-attribute whilst the ego continues to judge and never see that you are already all you need to be.

All these stories around being bold miss a fundamental truth. Despite our basic, egotistic fear, ('Am I loveable?' - A Course in Miracles,) we ARE love and we ARE loved. This is a truth any of us can feel when we set aside the ego, ignore the self-image and choose to listen to our own heart.

All those things for which we've believed we need to be bold are just a story told by our self-image, because it's only really our image of our self that can suffer.

You don't need to be bold. You just need to be willing to listen to your heart, and be willing to be you. Love is never conditional, you are loved as you already are.

# Preventing Miracles

Any grievance you hold is shielding you from oncoming miracles.

Whenever we are holding a grievance we are both judging and resisting reality. As Byron Katie says, every time we fight reality we lose. When we hold a grievance, we are resenting reality, we keep ourselves out of the flow of how things are, and it's only within that flow that miracles reveal themselves.

Once we surrender to 'what is' without judgment, and hence without resistance, once we give up our grievance and relinquish the judgmental thought that something even needs to be forgiven, as we move into loving acceptance, our energy changes and we become aligned with what the universe is offering us.

We start to notice the clues all around us, tokens of love miraculously appearing, little navigational signs that remind us 'yes, you are on your path.' Small miracles, sometimes wonderfully huge miracles, remind us that life loves us, just allow it. Allow.... allow... allow...

# No Reason to Be Angry

The reason for your anger was created by the source of your anger:

A thought.

Your reason for anger only exists as a thought, the creator of all reasons and meanings.

You think you have a reason to be angry.

You think the reason into existence.

The source of your anger is only ever and always a thought.

# Get Over Your Self

I'm not really interested in who you think you are.

Many coaches will work with you on your creation of some 'better self', have you work on being Batman rather than Robin, help you take your place at the top of some made up league table of comparison, and create beliefs that have you 'step into who you need to be' so that you can feel good, comfortable, or even confident when you think of yourself.

Confidence - a.k.a. the ability to have your self-critic shut the f**k up for a while. Very important, should you ever choose to listen to your self-critic...

You can expend much effort and growth in creating a new world for yourself which ultimately has its foundation built upon a new version of the image you have of yourself. Creating a new you so often only means creating a new self-image. For many this will serve a great purpose. If you've had 'low self-esteem' (basically a low opinion of your 'self', a less-than complimentary image of your 'self') why not create a more loving and better one?

Occasionally some might suggest you should display more aspects of your self, masqueraded as being vulnerable. Yet, is it truly vulnerable to display your self-image in a way that might have it exposed to being attacked or destroyed? There's only one person who cares about your self-image, and the clue is in the name. To everyone else it doesn't even exist. How can the non-existent be vulnerable?

Lady Gaga laying in a wild safari park whilst wearing her meat dress. Now, that's vulnerable!

Many coaches will work with you to have you feel more courageous, exert much effort to grapple and overcome all your made-up fears. Yet fears can only exist within the realm of a self-image and ego. Courage is only as real as the fear that demands it. Without fear, courage is an unnecessary concept that many use to continue to work on themselves, their self, as some self-created, self-centric, self-improvement project.

Self, self, self, self, self....

All this work on your image of your self will always be a never-ending project. The part of you that judges you and creates an image of you is only capable of judgement. Your self-image can only judge because it is only made of judgement. As you break through one layer so another will appear. If you decide you are Batman, your self-image will judge you as Batman.

Yet you are not your self-image.

The cake is not what you think of the cake. Why work on what you think of the cake?

Some coaches might even have you go back into the story of your past and talk with the image you had of yourself as a child. 'Let's take some time to look back at when you first formed this opinion of the cake.'

Does that even make sense to you?

There is only one person you need to be in this world. That's the person who is you when you are not trying to be somebody, who you are when you are not even trying to be some created vision of yourself.

What's it like to be you when you are not trying to be somebody?

What's it like to be you without your 'made-up-self?'

Almost everyone whom I have asked this question answers emphatically: "Free!" Yes, freedom! Freedom from the self. Freedom from your opinion of your self.

Without any judgement of the self, what is left? Love.

Love is the freedom that is in your heart. Love is the wisdom already in your heart that will hold you and guide you, irrespective of what made-up opinion you have of yourself.

I invite you to stop believing your opinion of yourself even matters or needs to be fixed. It doesn't, if you choose to no longer have it be any concern of yours. If you choose to listen to your heart instead.

Get over (the image you have of) your self.

*Curiosity is love.*

# I'm The Biggest Distraction in My Life

There's so much on offer that I can consider about myself, not least that very popular question in coaching circles, "Who do you need to be?"

In my experience this is perhaps one of the most distracting inquiries I can make before taking action, simply because it turns my focus away from the action I want to take and turns it in on myself, an area in which my ego has the most interest and investment. As part of this inquiry I've managed to move my focus away from something real that I want to create in the world, to a myriad of made-up unreal self-centeredness.

One of my most favourite things to do on this planet is sleep. I usually do it at least once a day, and quite frankly, if I don't I can be quite the bitch! But I've never stopped to consider "Who do I need to be to sleep?" That would just keep me awake!

If there is something I want to do, my most helpful inquiries are usually "What is the tiniest step I can take towards that now?" and "What can I LOVE about taking that action?"

I have a dear friend who's really into flowers and nature. If we pass some flowers, she'll often pause to smell them. I'm pretty sure she doesn't 'go inward' to consider who she needs to be to enjoy smelling the flowers. She's already doing what she loves. When she loves doing something it is not necessary to ask who she needs to be. The only thing she needs to be is present. Presence IS love.

The moment I start asking who I need to be I am caught up in an illusion that I'm some kind of big deal in taking action. That is fraught with noisy thinking because our egos want to believe we are a big deal at the same time as telling us we're not. So much noise!

Love is the only big deal.

I don't want to help people work out who they need to be in order to do something. I want to help them see that the reason they're not doing something is because they've not connected to loving doing it.

I want to help people see they are already everything and all they need to be to give anything a shot, and it's only the omming and sitting on their arses self-obsessively working out who they need to be that keeps them from taking action and being of service.

If you simply do what you love, your true essence of love will shine through. It's inevitable. There is nothing for you to do in order to work out who you need to be, you are already it - Love!

The problem with trying to work out who you are and who to be is that you can only consciously consider that inquiry in formed thoughts, thoughts that you can only consider intellectually. Yet who you are is not from form, it is from the formless energy of life, of love.

When you stop being distracted by your self-image, when you stop trying to work out who you are and who you need to be, and instead allow your love to flow, you'll soon see who you already are is all you ever need to be.

# Studying Success

When I've studied success I've often found I was actually studying egotistic acquisition and manipulation, along with a building and maintaining of me and my self-image.

When I've studied love and happiness I have invariably found I'm also actually studying success.

Funny that...

# The Normality of Truth

I recently shared with a friend some correspondence I had written to a very well-known coach. I wrote to the coach to tell him I felt he had misrepresented a conversation we'd had, and wrote without asking anything of him, simply expressing how I saw the situation. I also shared with my friend the message I had sent to the same coach after he had invited me to join a new program he had put together. Perhaps I was less than complimentary, but I was once again expressing what I felt was true for me and what I saw.

My friend replied to me: "Your level of honesty with him is commendable."

I disagreed.

It's unsavoury that we live in a world where someone expressing what they feel to be true is treated with praise, yet embellishments are accepted without any acknowledgment.

In my correspondence to this coach, following his invite to a new program, part of the feedback I gave was that, as I read through what he had sent, I found myself asking 'where is the love in this?' The coach's reply was simple - 'I'm sorry you're not seeing the love that's being created.'

That may have been true, of course, but what I actually sensed in his response was a defensive stance, rather than one of compassion and willing to teach love. A short while later I was removed from one of his groups, despite being assured earlier that I could remain, after it was decided I'd no longer be an ambassador for this particular group program.

We seem to live in a world where honesty, truth and speaking of how we feel is judged to be worthy of commendation, of particular recognition, yet hiding and being less than economical with our truth is considered usual. To such an extent that for some of us we fail to see the natural beauty and opportunity for loving connection when someone openly expresses their feelings, and take things personally instead.

A few months later I watched a couple of videos of this very same coach, where he suggested in the video that it was I who had asked to talk with him, and later that I had been dreaming about him and called him up to discuss this particular issue when, in reality, he had asked to talk to me about it. The embellishment was subtle, as they so often are. My challenge to him via email was met with simply being blocked on Facebook. The ultimate Hell-No!

In some ways, I can understand this stance, him choosing to not have what he saw as negativity in his life.

However, I see it quite differently. In a profession that many claim is all about helping our clients discover what is true for them, and calling them out on their bullshit, any coach worth his salt should be open to having his own embellishments and bullshit challenged too, and be willing to respond with curiosity and love.

Truth is a normality which many of us look to avoid through our fears.

Being open and willing to look at our own fears, bullshit and embellishment when challenged, now that just might be commendable.

# Ending It All

Michael (not his real name) came to see me, having been feeling very low, lost and noticing his thoughts about ending it all.

I'm always excited when someone comes to me with that kind of desire. I can see through the misunderstanding. It is not 'all' that they want to end. Just the suffering. Sadly, for many, suicide seems like the only way to do that.

A desire to end suffering. We're already on the same page.

Michael revealed another key ingredient we could use in cooking up a solution to this problem. He said "I've come to you because I think you can help me." He may have said "I know…" but that would have also been a misunderstanding. He couldn't yet know if I could help him. I hadn't helped him yet.

But he was willing to explore the possibility that I could help him. Again, we're on the same page.

Michael told many stories of how his boss had been treating him, the unreasonable expectations that his boss placed upon him, and that the constant battle was draining his energy and dragging him down through bouts of anger and frustration. I could see, as he relayed some of these stories, he was feeling distraught, even now.

Even now. When his boss wasn't even in the room with us. Even now, when his boss was probably at home, sitting on his sofa with his wife, paying no attention to whether Michael was following the unreasonable rules or not.

I pointed this out to Michael, that he seemed to be feeling all of this without his boss being present. Where did it seem those feelings were coming from? Surely, they couldn't be coming from his boss? He wasn't here. There was NOTHING of his boss in the room with us. So where were those feelings coming from?

"Because I'm thinking about it" he said. Tears of laughter started to roll down his cheeks. In that moment, he saw that all of his suffering was only ever coming from what he thought about his boss.

Even when his boss was in the room.

A few weeks later I checked with him. His work colleagues had accused him of being on happy pills, such was the transformation of the guy that used to walk in the office with slumped shoulders. He wasn't on any medication at all. Not even the anti-depressants he was taking at the time of our first conversation.

He didn't need to end it all. He didn't need any happy pills. He didn't need anything. Least of all to believe his thoughts about his boss.

And in that moment the suffering ended by itself.

# The Illusion of Complexity

I'm realising the more I understand and am in touch with love, the less I like complexities. I'm tempted to say the less well I deal with complexities, but that's not true. A big part of coaching is exploring through perceived complexities to discover simple truths. Often the truth of love. I'm pretty good at that.

But I notice some people like to have life be complex, have things mean things, about themselves and about life, live with many rules, meanings, definitions, and conditions. That's not for me. I don't often entertain that level of self-importance.

That's not to say I don't respect other's rules for life. As someone who habitually inhabits the Enneagram at point 9, not wanting to upset the apple cart is my forte. Unconsciously, I'll often agree to anything for peace.

I still believe it's important and helpful to establish and agree upon the nature of any relationship, what is acceptable and what is not. In fact, it is in agreeing these terms that complexity is reduced and love is able to flow unabated, and expressed in agreed and appropriate ways. Life is all-in-all easier within simple agreements rather than navigating complex expectations.

If I'm willing to understand it is never the intention of my partner, or indeed anyone else with whom I have any kind of relationship, to have me be pissed, if I am willing to trust their love for me, when I catch myself feeling pissed it's a good indicator I am not understanding them.

Byron Katie says if you're not feeling love you're confused.

And that makes sense, since love is our true nature. Babies are often described as a bundle of love, without all the conditioning they are subjected to during the rest of their life. Things remain pretty simple for babies and young children.

Then sadly and very quickly we develop the habit of meaning and prediction. We start believing that because things have happened to us once, they will happen again in the future if we allow them. We develop our mental triggers that warn us "here it comes, that thing you predicted would happen again!" But very often our ability to predict the future via those triggers is appalling. And so, our system becomes yet more complex as we try to get even better at our predictions.

Phew! I'm tired just trying to explain that! Such hard work, resisting love. Where is the love? Hidden behind all those fear-created rules, triggers and complexities.

I've often talked with friends about their relationships and concluded "It doesn't have to be hard work." No relationship needs be hard work. I don't even subscribe to the "relationships have to be worked at" ethic, since if you come from a loving place, it is effortless. Part of that love is a knowing and trusting that your partner loves you too.

I love you. I can't not love you, despite what my own ego or indeed your ego might have to say on the matter. And I'm willing to believe the same of you.

If all behaviours are either an expression of love, or call for love, an appropriate response to any behaviour is always love.

When I'm pissed and my relationships feel complex, I've likely forgotten that.

# Don't Wait for Joy

Towards the end of my first marriage, after I had moved out and rented a place of my own, I was drinking quite heavily and experimenting with various drugs that I thought might help me to feel better. Of course, they never did.

Waking in the mornings with a black hole of emptiness, compounded by a thumping head, empty food cupboards and wrappers from of a twelve pack of potato crisps strewn around the house, wasn't helping at all.

One morning I woke and knew I needed different help. Actual help. Up until then I wanted to deal with this on my own because I saw that as finding my own way. I didn't want to ask anyone for help, but I knew it felt like I was actually losing my way. I was scared where I might end up, or indeed if I might end up altogether.

Without showering (which might have woken my ego) and shivering in a coat not entirely suited to the frosty morning, I walked down to the local bus depot where my friend was alleged to have cleaned buses for a living, (a mostly unproven rumour.) He invited me aboard his current hiding place, a broom strewn across the aisle, and I told him I wasn't in a good place. "No, you're on a fucking filthy bus at 6am in the morning!" he said.

And he knew what I meant. "We'll get you some help, mate," he assured me. I could instantly see the ridiculousness of the situation, and the breath of the big deal exhaled from me.

As I surrendered to accepting help I remember my dear friend Geoff hugging me, on that half clean bus, as I sobbed in both laughter and despair. Laughing at our ability to always laugh, laugher to the power of laughter, even at what felt like the most inappropriate time.

Except it wasn't. Laughter is such a magical and powerful medicine.

If you're going to laugh about something later, why wait?

*Let joy be your guide.*

# Recognising Truth

Ever been told or read something you didn't think you knew yet recognised it with a deep knowing as true?

This is something my clients experience often, as we explore how they are creating their experience of life and they 'discover' the principles behind their experience.

These kinds of insights are often met with the temptation to slap ourselves on the forehead, 'Doh! Of course! How did I not see that?'

Because whilst we may be seeing something for the first time as true, truth isn't something we learn; it is something we recognise.

Hence when someone talks about something we know to be true yet intellectually we might not have heard before, we have a sense of recognition and feel "Aha! yes, that feels true for me." Like we recognise a picture of an old friend from school.

We are all connected to a greater intelligence, the wisdom of love and life, and in that wisdom, is truth, which we already have within us.

Since truth is something any client will recognise, as a coach, we don't need to teach our clients anything. We only need help them in their exploration of what is true for them, and do so under the guidance of our own curiosity of how our clients think they are putting their lives together.

In that exploration, they'll discover and recognise they already know all they need to know. And that knowing truth is so often way beyond any explanation of the intellect.

# Easier Said Than Kind

Being kind to everyone is NOT easier said than done.

We so often allow those types of little statements, "It's easier said than done," to sneak into our conversations and thinking, yet they only ever come from fear.

Being kind IS easier done than not, because not being kind means we are caught up in an illusion of separateness and fear. That fear takes work and effort to maintain. Most of us spend a good proportion of our lives maintaining it, wondering what people will think of us, what they might 'do to us' or try to 'get from us!' Trying to predict a future from fear instead of trusting in and CHOOSING TO SEE the abundance of love in the universe.

Being love is what we truly are when we are not doing anything to maintain that illusion of separateness and fear. Being kind is our default from which only ego detours, when we are not caught in an illusion of lack. Being kind is the easiest way to be because it is, ultimately, who we are when we allow everything else to fall away.

You can choose not to believe your ego. You can choose not to believe your fears. You can choose to allow the unconditioned you to shine through your fears. You can choose to allow your default choice to be being kind.

# Grandparents

My grandparents both lived well into their nineties. They were married for over seventy years and lived in the same house for pretty much all of that time.

They lived a very simple life, never owned a car, were not into foreign holidays, lived in a very cosy house full of lots of laughter, fun and love. And they brought up three children, one of which is my dear Mother.

I realise, too, that they were the most spiritual people I have ever known, without ever having any kind of traditional spiritual conversation with them.

They'd rather talk about tea and cake than the Tao and kale. They didn't scrape their tongues clean in the mornings, they didn't drink warm water with lemon or have green smoothies with avocado and quinoa, I'm pretty sure they drank whilst standing up and didn't have a footstool whilst sitting on the loo. They ate cooked breakfasts, the fat off the ham, they put tea and coffee in their mouths rather than up their arses, a downward dog was taking their pet out for a walk down bishops hill, and visioning had something to do with cleaning their glasses before they played darts or cards.

I don't recall ever seeing my Grandma wearing heavy make-up to cover her beautiful natural face. I'm pretty sure my Grandad didn't spend hours in the gym to develop a six-pack. He was always more of a keg man, enjoying an occasional pint of his beloved Adnams ale.

They preferred to work at jobs rather than on themselves, my Grandma always cooking up some magic in the kitchen, my Grandad strong as an ox yet the most gentle and soft-hearted man that you could ever meet. He'd cry if his dear Annie was in any kind of pain, and distraught with tears when we said goodbye to each other for the final time, I thanked him for all the love in our family which felt like it came through him.

They were not concerned with the phases of the moon, numbers on clocks and doors, the energy of cats passing in the street, interplanetary orbits, or any behavioural strategies that took them out of now and hence away from each other.

Anything that happened in their pasts remained there, gone, without it having to define the enjoyment they got from simply being with each other in every moment in the present.

They didn't give a fuck about any of that stuff!

They simply loved each other.

And in that simplicity life was very long, very loving, so much fun, and mostly easy. They were never trying to be anybody, and in that they allowed it to be easy to love each other. Without so many of the complications many of us like to entertain today.

God-bless you Grandma & Pop. Always grateful for the reminder to come back to the simplicity of love

# The Miracle Has Already Occurred

Do you know the odds of you being you? There's been a few articles floating around illustrating these odds, gatrillions and trazillions to one chance of you being conceived as you, being born in your country, and living on this piece of rock that's spinning at a thousand miles an hour whilst travelling through space at 67,000 miles an hour.

The odds of you being you are almost inconceivable, you being you is miraculous!

And here you are, wishing for some miracle to bring you some amount of money, or some career move, or some other earthly occurrence that looks like a miracle.

The miracle has already occurred.

Once you are willing to embrace that, any tweaks around the edges of that miracle will become much more obvious and accessible to you.

# I Wish You Knew Just How Easy It Could Be

How many times have you said to yourself "wow, that was so much easier than I thought"? Certainly, in my experience it is most times after I have been telling myself something will be difficult. What unlocks it for me is not the simple act of taking action. There is something before that.

I'm noticing that I've written 'unlocks' because so often I've thought there must be some kind of key. Assuming something needed to be 'unlocked' I'd get right on the case of searching for that right key, the key that fitted, the one that slipped into the lock effortlessly and would turn as easily as a hot pin in butter. I've even got excited before conversations with my own coach, looking forward to finally discovering that final key point that I need to work through, that one piece of self-improvement, that one missing piece that has been holding me back

An endless search that could not possibly bear fruit since neither the key or indeed the lock actually exist.

As long as you search for something that does not exist I absolutely guarantee you will never find it.

But what a great distraction all that searching provides!

What 'unlocks' it for me before action? A very simple, subtle yet fundamental change in my thinking. Much like if you've ever tried to open a door, pushed or rammed against it only to discover that you were pushing the side with the hinges, or maybe you needed to pull rather than push, the simple change in thinking is usually for me not an actual change in thinking at all ('I need to open this damn door') but a willingness to let go of how seriously I am taking my thinking ('is that door real?")

Believing it is difficult is not the same as thinking it is difficult. Thinking is not the same as knowing. Believing is choosing to know.

I might think something is going to be so damn difficult I may as well not even attempt it. But only believing that thought keeps me out of action. Most times it really doesn't matter what I think because experience tells me most times I am wrong. Things are very usually much easier than I initially think.

What a great distraction all that thinking provides!

The decision to ignore my thinking takes many forms; it can be a simple 'fuck it, let's see what happens' or a 'who cares what I or others think' or maybe 'well, what's the worst that can happen? Would I be okay with that?' They all amount to the same approach, my indifference to my own thinking, mixed in with a sprinkling of adventure and willingness to 'screw up' (a.k.a. get unexpected results).

As humans, our ability to predict outcomes, timing or any aspect of the future is often appalling. But we can be masterful at being willing to allow the flow (often called 'going with the flow') to let things take the shape they will. When we stop lying to ourselves in our attempts to tell ourselves we do know what will happen or how difficult something will be, we are left with not knowing.

It's from that place of not knowing that adventure and magic comes.

Is not knowing scary? Maybe, if you think it is. You can also choose for it to be exciting.

And within that not knowing is still one FACT we have in our favour. Almost always things are so much easier than we initially think. If we look at the evidence of that, we can start to believe our next endeavour may also be easy. We can begin to know just how easy it could be.

# How Selfish of Me to Not Ask for Help

When I choose to not ask for help I am identifying with my own self-image of separation.

The sole function of the ego is to maintain an identity of a separate self, and hence ego sees asking for help as failure to maintain that separateness. The ego simply sees asking for help as failure.

My not asking for help can be an expression of my own unique separateness, validating my self-image, validating that I can do this alone, which is always a lie. Even the lone cactus in the desert needs the sun and a little rain.

I might also be afraid of how others see me or judge me in my asking. This is a fear that can only manifest in the realm of self-image, because I want you to see me a certain way - independent, strong, or even considerate in not bothering you.

In keeping you out, I keep my true essence in, and ultimately feel disconnected from you, the universe, and from love.

Only my self-obsession stops me asking for help, and only my self-obsession keeps me disconnected from love.

Yet my heart knows asking for help is an expression of unity and is an invitation for participation. My asking is an acknowledgment that we're both already at the dance party, even if you don't want to share this particular dance. We're already part of the dance, we're both already dancing with the universe.

Should I be declined my heart knows it cannot be a reflection of me because I am not separate from you. I need not fear not being loved because I know you, and I, are love.

My ego sees asking for help as failure.

My heart sees it as an invitation of unity, participation and love.

*You are the one you've been waiting for.*

# There's Always Shit Going Down

Life is always happening, all around us and around the world. As well as conflict, natural disasters, political injustices and family differences, there's always some planet in retrograde whilst we're subjected to various eclipses and moon phases.

Each of us always has the capacity and ability to rise above all these outside circumstances, irrespective of how compelling it might seem that they affect us inside. Even if you believe the alignment of planets, moons, stars and weather can affect our moods, we always have the capacity and ability to vibrate higher than our moods, higher than our thinking and all that is going on around us and outside of us.

Throughout history there are stories of people rising above immense personal trauma or challenge. Choosing to be an owner rather than victim. We all have that within us.

In any moment, I can choose to be either a victim of my mood, the weather or the moon, or become an owner of how I want to live my life. In any moment, I can realise my potential to feel love and rise above all the shit that is always happening around me, and sometimes feel like it is happening within me.

Love is the energy of creation. In love, I can always create. In love, I can always rise. Whatever shit is going down.

# "Freedom's just another word for nothing left to lose..."

How free do we really want to be?

Freedom. Seems to be mentioned in just about every other blog or Facebook post. Maybe freedom is the new 6-figures. Maybe freedom is the new black.

The way I see it, only a few of us would be doing things very differently if we realised our freedom. Despite the stories we tell ourselves, we're all pretty much doing what we want to do, in any given moment. Not because we don't realise how free we already are, but because freedom isn't really what we want.

Freedom is just another 'in order to.'

We want freedom in order to do something differently. And believe what we'd do differently would help us be happy.

I call bullshit!

Freedom is just another conceptualised container for happiness and joy. The difference between it and many other quests, such as 6-figures or the perfect partner, is that you already have freedom, in so much as you are always choosing what to do and how to respond, and when to feel happy.

Only those that have realised this feel free.

The rest of us are like fish in a river looking for water.

I say screw the quest for freedom! It's a distraction from what every single one of us really wants: Joy.

Can there be a greater reason for doing something other than joy? Is there a more worthwhile cause than the expansion of love and happiness?

Joy is at the end of the 'in-order-to' line. Joy, happiness, love, ARE the point of everything.

Please let joy be the new black. It's a much more obvious attribute of the human experience than freedom, and it's as contagious as head-lice at a wig-sharing party.

Let's get straight to the point and drop all the 'in order to' BS.

Let's drop the distractions and get straight to joy.

# Choose Choice

Until I have chosen I will always be deciding. Deciding is exhausting!

Choosing, however, is liberating. Once I've chosen I can just chuffing get on with it...

Whilst in the process of deciding I'll take notice of all things that are in favour of my decision, and when something good happens I'll use that to 'prove' my deciding process of being in favour.

Whilst in the process of deciding I'll take notice of all things that are against, and when something bad happens I'll use that to 'prove' my deciding process of being against.

Whilst this is going on I'll fill my head with thinking, reasons to, reasons not to. A constant little battle going on up there.

And all this time I'll remain a victim to all outside influences, like a damp pair of grey underpants hanging out on a washing line, swaying in the wind.

Once I have chosen I am free from so much thinking, and I can enjoy all the pros, and simply see any cons as circumstances to be danced around. Like driving to the airport whatever the weather.

If I want something I only need choose it.

Stop being imprisoned by deciding.

Choose and be free.

# Believing Like I'm a Rapist

Believing I need to change external circumstances to change how I feel is a similar strategy to having women dress differently to avoid being raped.

Whoah! How can that be so?

The fundamental reason someone commits the atrocious act of rape, or indeed any other hideous crime such as acts of terror, is simply this: They believe they must act on a thought.

This is the same fundamental truth that has any of us behave in ways such as opening the fridge door at 11pm, or checking our phones by the bed or in a restaurant.

Just like having women dress differently to avoid being raped, we can put locks on our fridge doors or charge our phones in our kitchens. These all fit into the 'avoid the temptation' strategy by making it more difficult to act on the thought "I must eat now," or "I must attack and have sex now."

And of course, there are circumstances when such strategies may seem the most sensible option, but each are a distraction from the true cause of these behaviours, and therefore a missed opportunity to create real change in our world.

Once we see that we do not have to believe our thoughts and do not have to take action on them, we no longer need the lock on the fridge door or to move our phones away from us when we are with a group of friends.

I doubt many of us think we should change the circumstances in which people live to stop potential rapists believing thoughts that they think mean they must commit such appalling acts.

Yet we'll happily proliferate a misunderstanding that we must change our circumstances to feel and behave differently in other ways. It's not true for women in short skirts and rapists, and it's not true for moving your phone to the kitchen.

Just as I don't believe I really should ram my car into the guy who just cut me off in traffic, I can also choose not to believe my thought that says I should check my phone now.

Once we see that we do not have to believe any of our thoughts that attempt to tell us how to behave, we are free of the constant quest to change our circumstances to fit our thinking.

We're no longer a prisoner of our thinking and our circumstances. We become free of both.

That is the liberation I want to teach our children.

# Change Isn't Always as Good as a Rest

Buying new toilet rolls because they looked nice and had 'Shea butter' (dafuq is that for in toilet rolls???) has been a total disaster. I'm sure you don't want me to go into the details but let's just say they fail in ways you really don't want toilet rolls to fail.

Way back when I was on my apprenticeship in my I.T. career, I guess at this time I was about 18 years old, I was working in a computer room that was being used to test BT's video on demand system. We used to load massive laser discs into room-size arrays of players, all connected to a computer system that filled another room.

The guy I was working with, a wise old Indian man, was responsible for the day to day operations of the computer system, and for all his work he used one of the original computer terminals. For the tech geeks, it was an original DEC VT100, a big, heavyweight thing with keys that almost needed a hammer to operate.

I asked him "Why don't you upgrade to a new terminal, such as a VT220?" The VT220 was the latest, and hence greatest, terminal around, and some of his colleagues used them. It was oh so much smaller and lighter. His response has stuck with me since.

"Would you change your wife just because there is a younger, lighter one around?" I laughed so hard. He continued into a mini rant about how this was what was wrong with the world, how "everyone wants to trade-up all the time, rather than simply loving what they already have."

And he really did love that old computer terminal.

This was back in the mid 80s. I had not even realised my interest in personal growth and human behaviour at that time. I hadn't even met my future wife from whom I was to learn so much when our marriage eventually did break down (despite my clinging on to it for much longer than was good for any of us in it.)

And I could see the wisdom in what he said so clearly, even then.

Maybe the impact of those few words helped me stay loyal and want to fight to keep something that was, on reflection, past it's time. My commitment and loyalty was actually immense in that marriage, even at times trying to type on a computer terminal that, perhaps, had no display.

How do we square that with wanting to make the world a better place?

Knowing when it's time to upgrade your terminal because it is dead is not the same as being drawn to a new one because it simply looks better. That is a strategy of fear, fear of missing out.

And accepting and loving what is gives us access to an inner peace that guides us to make changes in the world in a loving way.

# Don't be a Thought Terrorist

"How can you be so happy when people are dying, being bombed and murdered?"

A common question. And I can see the sense in it. With so much going on in the world today, a world where acts of terrorism anywhere are reported immediately the world over, we can find plenty of reasons to put aside our love and happiness and choose fear, hatred and sadness instead.

Yet if we choose fear, the terrorists have won. They will have succeeded in their quest to proliferate terror. If we choose to live in terror and act upon it we have become an agent of the change the terrorists seek.

Of course, each and every time I hear of any such acts I do feel sad, and occasionally anger too.

In any moment we can feel sad, but we need not BE sad.

In immersing myself in this work I have become much more masterful at catching my own fearful thinking and letting it go. Just like the terrorists I can choose whether to believe my fearful thinking. Unlike the terrorists, I choose not to.

In a world where we now get to see so much fear, hatred and sadness, we must be even more determined to be lights of love and happiness. Martin Luther King, Jr. summed this up beautifully - "Darkness cannot drive out darkness; only light can do that. Hate cannot drive out hate; only love can do that."

Empathy need not be an act of sacrifice, it can be an act of love.

With each act of terror, I am more determined to spread happiness, I am more determined to love.

Instead of being a thought terrorist I choose to be a light of love and happiness.

*Love has power beyond our comprehension.*

# About to...

Did you hear about the guy who went to his twenty seventh workshop on living in the present? He'd just finished studying his fortieth book that year, managed to squeeze in all that reading about how to create his perfect future between a series of webinars and YouTube videos on how to get over your past.

Once again, he said "Oh I got so much out of this, I can feel something coming through for me..."

There it was again. Coming...

As in... not here yet...

Coming... about to...

Like a constipated toad staring at his pack of Senakot...

About to take them...

But... ....just.....

...not... yet...

So not now....

I guess he'll be going to another workshop sometime soon... Maybe after he's worked through all of his Facebook saved list  Oh, and then there's that book that Bob wrote about in his post, what was it? How to blog on the bog, get rid of your fog, sleep like a log...

Or was it a podcast? Life goes so fast...

Maybe he needed to sleep on what it was that was coming through  about his latest insight...  He'd soon be in touch with what he already knew  And accept what he didn't... He might consider that inquiry with the morning dew...

Sometime in the future... It was coming... like the future always is...

Never in the ONLY moment he is ever living, not this.

Not this living moment. Or that one just gone.

He'd delay his living moment until the infinite span of the future actually arrived.

Maybe, although unlikely, sometime before his grave...

Almost, but never now.

# Stepping on Toes

Sometimes it's as crazy to do nothing as it is do something. Either way, avoiding crazy is a great strategy for avoiding life. Many of my most fun memories have me roar in laughter at the crazy times.

As the message of 'Do nothing' is proliferated to help people live in peace, its misinterpretation often has us die before we're dead. I fell into this chasm of an intellectualised peace that subdued my heart's desire to live. Then was woken with a jolt and exclamation - "No! This is NOT how my heart wants to live life!"

Do nothing, from the head

Ignore the heart, just play dead

Ah, to be! To be free as me!

Alive in all its guises, in all life's mystery.

There I was, living with a quest for peace, in itself a contradiction, instead of being at peace with allowing all of me. But what of the risks of being me?

Maybe there are no risks, just miscalculated consequences, some of which we are not willing to bare.

Oh but if we are, how free we become! To dance in the craziness of it all, in whirlwinds of heart's desires and misguided adventures. Creating stories for our children's children. Creating our most colourful wake.

We can spend our life as a wallflower trying to work out the right thing to do, or we can be willing to be part of the dance, and step on toes whilst our feet find our hearts.

We can be a wallflower laughing at the dancers. Or be a dancer creating laughter and inspiring the wallflowers.

# Fun is your Time Machine

Do you ever look back at something fun that happened and feel surprised at just how long ago it was? Oh, that party where uncle Geoff played air-guitar naked on the table in the restaurant, wow, was that really fifteen years ago? It feels like fifteen minutes! I can still smell the fire extinguisher spray...

Yet when we look back at what felt like tough times, often they don't bring the same surprise. "Oh gosh, that was soooo long ago, and yes, it was tough; I'd never put up with that for so long now. Who the hell was that guy who did that?"

I often have a sense of wondering who on earth it was who stayed in a relationship or allowed his life to be what it was for so long. Like it was some imposter living my life back then compared to the person I am now.

I'm wondering if the reason for this is that not only do we learn and grow from 'tough times,' they also represent times in our lives when we have forgotten who we are. Maybe that's why, once we are through with them, they seem so much further away.

It seems to make sense, then that fun times ARE a reflection of who we are, hence they feel so recent, so much closer and much more connected to how we see ourselves today.

Are you allowing fun to be part of your life?

Are you allowing you?

# Pacman

Do you remember Pacman? The little creature that you directed around the screen to collect pills? Of course, those pills weren't real, they were just coloured dots on the screen. And then, of course, (spoiler alert!) Pacman wasn't real either.

But it was fun. Simple fun. Collect so many pills and you advanced to a new level. And at each level things got a little more difficult. That didn't matter, of course, because the point of the game was to advance through those levels.

I've never met anyone who got to the end of the game, who 'completed Pacman'

I'm not even sure if there was an end...

The thought occurred to me during a conversation recently that some of us see life a bit like the game of Pacman, with our self-image playing the main character. Often, we think that image is real and needs to be fed, so we direct it around looking for pills.

Pills for enlightenment, pills for freedom, pills for courage or vulnerability, pills for awesomeness, pills for anything and everything that the image of ourselves tells us we need.

We might move through supposed levels, but that self-image is never satisfied. It always wants more and another level is necessary.

If we believed the game of Pacman to be real we'd suffer because at some point the character failed, got caught or eaten by ghosts, and we either started that level again or died.

Life really can look like that too. But only if we forget it is a game and none of the ghosts, levels or pills are real.

I loved playing Pacman, and always knew it was just a game. I got quite good at it because I played it for fun.

And sometimes I forget to play life like that too.

# No Second Chances

Don't give second chances. They're so loaded with the past.

Not even another chance. That carries too, the weight of previous chances past and missed.

We all screw up. Many screw-ups are about withholding a part of ourselves - "I can't show that, yet, so take this made-up piece instead."

Not allowing your truth is always a screw-up.

And we all do it.

Everyone.

We're all scared of showing ourselves. We don't always take the first or thirty-second chance to do so.

If you are in the business of giving people chances, love them at least until they show themselves. Then love them more.

If you're in the business of taking chances, show yourself, unaudited, unadulterated, show you. Whenever you get the chance.

And if you're like the rest of us, seize your new chance. And give a new chance.

Keep giving chances until you see the real love.

Keep taking chances until you express your true love.

Oh, how we love a new chance...

# Fuck You! = Fuck Me!

Self-love is never about disregarding everyone or someone else. The act of loving yourself can never include having no regard for another's feelings as a result of your actions.

Self-love is a recognition in seeing your true essence as love, seeing the self as love. In that recognition, nothing need change. There is no prescription in self-love, only recognition. If your prescription of self-love is "I'm going to love myself so fuck you!" or any other version of disregard for another's feelings, it's not an act of love, and therefore cannot be from your true essence of love. If it's not from your true self it can only be an act from your ego self, and in that be an act of fear, not love.

Similarly, disregard for yourself in any act of love is not a reflection of your true essence, and cannot truly be an act of love. Any sacrifice you make is an attempt to separate yourself from love.

Yet love is not some balancing act between ourselves and others. It is harmonious and inclusive. What we want for others we must also want for ourselves. What we give to others we also give to ourselves.

There is no separation between ourselves and others in acts of love.

*The world looks the way it does because you're looking at it that way.*

# Walking

You're walking downtown, earphones in, podcast or music in full swing, and you're running a little late. Across the other side of the street you see someone you know. But it's not someone you particularly like or enjoy spending time with. You're just too different in how you see the world, you just don't have any kind of deep connection with them. So, you pretend you've not seen them, keep your eyes straight ahead and carry on walking.

We've all done it, or something similar, right?

If I told you I did this I am guessing you don't have particularly much judgment about it. You could probably enter into some dialogue with me how my actions were justified, i.e. make a positive judgment about it.

But what if that person was a close relative. Like your own father, for example? Is the judgment different? I've certainly experienced a lot of judgement around this when I've discussed this kind of thing with friends.

The judgment comes from all the conditioning we have about how we 'should' feel about our parents or other relatives. Now, some 'in the know' might say 'good for you, I wouldn't want to speak to that idiot either!' Or perhaps something less kind. But I'm never looking for that kind of solidarity. I'm not carrying the kind of bitterness that kind of sentiment carries.

One of the hardest things some of us have to deal with is coming to a realisation that one of our parents isn't really the kind of person we aspire to or even like. We're conditioned to look up to our parents. Yet they are just fallible human beings like the rest of us.

When I get into a deeper discussion about how I feel about my own father it often baffles people. Some listen to understand, and eventually do get some insight into the freedom I have realised. And it IS a wonderful, peaceful feeling I have around it. Others often can't see past their own deep conditioning of how we should treat or feel about our parents.

My father was a very good provider when we were kids. He worked incredibly hard, often had two jobs, and whilst we were at the lower end of the working-class scale with few luxuries, we didn't go without anything we needed.

And frankly he was very poor at connecting with us children, and often abusive to us kids and our Mum.

And he was always doing the best he could in the moment. I've no doubt he was struggling with his own stuff, being a provider and parent, and also needed more love in his life.

Him disowning me for ten years was him doing what he thought was the right thing to do, in the moment, just like the rest of us.

I did a lot of work around this. Through counselling and self-exploration, and more so recently into gaining a deeper understanding of love. I have learnt so much about life, being a parent, and about love from my father.

And my understanding and being at peace with that does not mean I have to go visit him, hug him and hang out with him any more than anyone else in my life. I owe my father nothing, he owes me nothing. Not even an apology, although he has offered one in the last few years. Anyone who thinks otherwise is being influenced by their own conditioning of how we should be with our parents.

Spoiler Alert: We're free to hang out and be with whoever we choose, irrespective of past conditioning.

Life is precious. I don't hang around with people I don't like. I don't like my Dad much, although I find with age we are both softening. We're just too different in many ways. I visit him, but often catch myself feeling obligation rather than preference. One of my own mentors suggested to me last year that doing something for someone else out of obligation probably isn't coming from love.

I also love my Dad. But it is no longer bound by the conditioning of how we should feel about our parents. I am genuinely free from that. And I have no bitterness, either. I am free of that too. So, I love him just as I love the homeless guy who often sleeps under a shelter near my home. To me they deserve the same love and attention. There is no difference. There is no separation. When I believe there is, I set up conditions for love and peace, of which there really are none.

It's fascinating to witness people's reaction to this deeper level of understanding of love. The unconditional nature of it all. How the 'shoulds' creep in. "Yes, but he's your Dad!" they'll say. "And so what?" I'll say. Cue discussion that's essentially about transactions - he did this for you so you should do that for him.

Love is not transactional. Love is freedom.

Another reaction when I share this with others is often one of sadness. I'm fascinated by that, too, since it also comes from the same conditioning and hence lack of realisation of freedom.

Personally, I don't feel sad about it. I feel the joyous freedom that is available to all of us. I feel the liberation of letting go of all the conditioning and expectations.

Anita Moorjani's book, Dying to be Me, continues to influence me in this way, knowing that on the other side we really are all one. The homeless guy, our parents, our abusers. We can love them all the same. In fact, we do love them all the same, it's only our conditioning that tells us otherwise. All part of our self-image that we use to project how we think we should love.

If you love spending time with your parents, your friends, your relatives, go do that! Be in that joy. We're always free to follow our joy. But if you don't, it's not loving to sacrifice your time to do so. There is no liberation or love in imprisoning yourself in relationships that are not joyous for you, irrespective of the conditions of obligation.

Any time we sacrifice our joy is an attempt to separate ourselves from love.

We're already free.  Love is that freedom.  Free to spend time with whoever we choose.

And free to keep walking too.

# The Day It All Changed

I heard the screaming, the shouting, the pandemonium, as shock took over my body for a few moments, wondering what on earth I might find as I went upstairs. My mother was crying, "No! No! No!" as if she had found my father dead. In a way, she had.

I had a very uneventful childhood, or at least so I thought up to that night when, aged sixteen, the marriage of my parents came to an abrupt end. Up until then we had all been asleep. Except my father. He had been either awake or at least dreaming of a new life of being awake.

So often he would come home from work and have his dinner separate from us, then retire to his chair, the one that had its back to us, and escape his monotonous life with his family by wearing headphones. My mother would often shout at him and bang on the floor to grab his attention; he'd very reluctantly raise one headphone off his right ear and exclaim "What now?"

The night he told my mother he loved someone else and wanted to leave us changed the sleepy, cruising course of all of our family. It impacted so many of us, including my uncles and grandparents. It felt so abrupt, yet as the immediate years passed, we came to see it was actually where we'd all been heading all along.

As I sat on the bottom of my parent's bed, I could hear my mother crying in another room.

"So, what's her name?" I asked my Dad.

I did have a bit of a temper when I was a kid, but mostly only when I felt incredible frustration with my brother and his teasing or aggravating. I just wanted life to be peaceful and wanted to be loved. I so wanted to fit in, particularly at school and amongst friends. (A very typical enneagram type nine, by the way.) When I think now of that boy who detested any kind of upset or violence, I feel a great empathy. Things certainly went awry after that night but, up to that point, I suspect I was the most grounded of our family. The thinker, the observer, the lover. I remember many times pondering if I was perhaps the second coming, if I was in fact Jesus and was here to bring love. My mother tells me she allowed herself to enjoy my childhood more than any of my siblings. The others brought the steep learning curve of a firstborn, followed by the arrival of twins two years later, which meant 'busy' was simply how my mother breathed. I arrived after a three and half year break and we had lots of time together alone as my other siblings were at school.

I was the one who brought peace.

"Joan," my father told me.

Joan. The name of the woman who would refuse to allow me to speak to my father for many years. Joan. The name of the woman who would drive a stake in-between my father and his own parents and have him disown them until after his own father was dead and buried.

"Joan. I thought you might understand," he said.

"These things happen," I said. "I think you have to do what you want to do."

As we all settled down for the night, a million movies playing though our minds of how things might be, I lay on the top bunk bed of my and my brother's room. I slept in his bed as he was staying the night with his girlfriend and my mother lay on the bottom bunk.

I allowed a hand to drop over the side of the bed and invited her to hold it.

"It'll all be okay, Mum," I told her.

The next fourteen years were at least as traumatic as the previous had been seemingly uneventful. My old-school pattern of being a loner had me compromise in relationships, jump into a crazy, abusive marriage, play with drugs and lots of alcohol, attempt suicide and dive into depression. So many experiences, but ultimately not very loving times. When I look back at them, I don't even recognise the guy who was living them.

My mother reinvented herself after that night, and I'm happy to report that it was without doubt the best thing that could have happened to her. She found herself and her own self-expression, and built a life with a wonderful, attentive and loving man who epitomises peaceful living. They have been happily married for over twenty-five years.

The grounded love the sixteen-year-old boy showed that night may have marked the last time for a while I was truly myself. When I consider him now, I see how I neglected him during my late teens and throughout my twenties, how I ignored him and lost him. Fortunately, the earth tremor and jolt of my marriage finally collapsing meant I started to really look into human behaviour and how I personally had behaved, and after much exploring, I've gotten him back. I've gotten me back. The grounded observer, the peacemaker, the lover. That sabbatical into a crazy wilderness brought me many incredible lessons and much wisdom, but the journey since those crazy times has been so much more beautiful. The lover loves more.

In writing this, I have realised we don't love for reward. It's not something I had even considered until now, but I notice how I see that what happened during the fourteen years of my life after my father left our family was nothing to do with how loving I was on that night, or any other time. What happened whilst I got lost doesn't have to have any reason or meaning. It just is.

There is no balance sheet for love.

We love because we are love. It's who we are.

# Sing

Don't let the time pass with things unsaid.
Don't just hum the tune when the words are in your
head.
Allow all in your heart to be seen and felt.
Let the warmth of your love have others egos melt.

Behind that shadow of yourself we know you are real
Share with us what you have to say, share with us how
you feel
Hold our hands, in fear, in sadness, in joy and delight
Embrace our hearts, light our souls in the darkness of
our night

As we wake each morning, glisten with the summer dew
You are here with a message; the message is you.
Wherever or whoever, let us all know your dance.
Smile, kiss, show your kindness, at every chance.

For when your time has come and you are gone
If you sang it to us, we'll all still sing your song.

# When Did You Last Love Yourself?

No, this question is not meant as an invasion into your intimate private life. When did you truly feel connected to the love you have for yourself?

Many people considering this question will see self-love as an activity, as something 'to do.' Some will also believe it's something we need to 'do more of and more often.' Pondering the self-love question, we often think of it as something to undertake to balance out some unkind acts against ourselves, such as when we are less than complimentary to ourselves, when we ignore or play down our own needs, feel angry at ourselves for supposed failures or mistakes, or beat ourselves up and run ourselves down.

Self-love becomes yet another burdensome activity for us to fit in our to-do list, some 'me-time' we might reluctantly add to our schedule.

Yet there is an alternative way of seeing self-love that requires you to do absolutely nothing. (My favourite kind of realisation!)

Whenever I talk to people about self-love they often talk about activities they undertake to 'make up for' what they have put themselves through, or some kind of reward for what 'life has thrown at them.' A congratulatory self-hug for managing to get through a tiring day getting the kids back to school, or an extra special treat for eating healthy all week. Just as a lack of self-love manifests in many ways, there's at least as many activities we are willing to embark upon to offer ourselves some 'much needed' affection, congratulation and approval.

But approval is not acceptance. Most acts of self-love are tokens of approval, gifts of deservedness. Yet if I approve of something (or someone) I am still making a judgment against some standard, which infers that should it not be met, I would disapprove. Approval and disapproval are two sides of the same coin.

Approval isn't love. Approval is another judgment.

So often we run from one end of the seesaw of judgment to the other, playing a drama game within our self-image of trying to balance out times when we are hard on ourselves with times when we are less so. Reward becomes just the other side of the coin of judgment and deservedness. We may be harsh on ourselves on one side, and so reward ourselves on the other. Reward becomes part of a negotiation, often a kind of contractual, conditional remuneration.

Yet when we are in touch with love there is a natural equilibrium, an acceptance beyond judgment.

By all means, have the dark Belgium chocolates, buy yourself red roses, treat yourself to a massage, get down to the gym and feast on spinach soup for lunch. Allow yourself some quiet time, say f**k it and book that holiday, have a sit-down with a cup of tea, get a manicure and buy the not-from-concentrate juice. Wear cashmere, go walk bare-foot on the sand, take a candle-lit bath with your favourite novel, even stay in bed an extra hour and forgive yourself of all ills.

I invite you to enjoy all physical pleasures available to us in this wonderful world. Indulge your senses.

Yet if you listen to your judgments of yourself you are not in touch with what you already are – Love.

Love does not judge. Love does not condemn and hence love does not ever need to forgive or reward. Self-Love is an unconditional, absolute acceptance of all of you.

You don't need to reward yourself as part of some negotiation of affection for yourself. Any act of self-reward to counterbalance judgment is not an act of love. Love needs no action or negotiation of judgment. Love is the absence of judgment.

That part of us – love – is ever-present, obscured only by the image we create of ourselves that tries to dictate whether we deserve something or not. Love is only ever obscured by a self-image. Without self-image, there is only love.

And as for the question, 'When did you last love yourself?' – You have never not loved yourself, because you are love. You are it, the lover and the loved.

Self-love is not so much an activity as a recognition of who you really are.

If you're willing to allow the self-critic to fade and feel yourself drop down into your heart, you may recognise love as the true you. That part of you is not only available atop a misty Indian mountain; it is with you always. Even in the supermarket as you fight back a scream because you left your shopping list at home.

I'd like to extend an invitation to you that one of my mentors, Robert Holden, offered to me. I invite you to allow yourself to notice the judgments without choosing to be the judge. Simply notice them pass through without adding yet another layer of judgment about them. And in simply noticing them, in allowing them without resistance, you may find some acceptance of who you are, and feel the self-love that is already you, Belgium chocolates optional.

# Why Wait?

How wonderful might it be to acknowledge, honour and show love to those still alive and still with us, as much as we so often do for those who have just passed...

To hold them and hug them a little more, to tell them we love and appreciate them, whilst they are still around to share.

How beautiful to be awake to our love for others before we meet at their wake.

To press the pause button on our own life and often self-obsession, to reflect on what their presence means to us, just as we might if they suddenly left, and to share that with them whilst they are here to hear.

How lovingly abundant it would feel to allow the gratitude for those we love and cherish whilst we may still hold them dear, without the underlying feeling of loss that arises when they are gone.

Instead of a tipping of our hat to the stars or posthumously posting something they said or a favourite song, what if we embraced them and celebrated them, gifted them our loving kindness and appreciation for them being alive, let them know that everything between us is always okay.

What if there was nothing unsaid when they, or we, are dead, because we allowed our love to be freely expressed, in the sweetness of every day.

What if love was always an expression in the present.

Who would you hug, who would you call?

Who would you ask to pause for a moment whilst you held their hands and looked in their eyes

To see them, feel them, be with them, without fear or regret.

Instead of waiting for the final goodbye, we simply called to say 'Hi'

'I love you. I love you. Thank you.'

*There's a lot of space to enjoy between never and always.*

# We're Never Not Creating

Most of us interested in human behaviour or psychology will have come across the concept that we create our own reality. Delving a little deeper into this we can see that whatever is going on in the physical world around us, it is indeed us that is creating our experience of that world through the principle of thought.

Any moment we're having an experience, we're creating it.

If you are anything like me (stop resisting, I know you are!) you will have had times when you just don't feel creative. You might find yourself sitting in front of a blank screen, in a huff on the sofa, or employing any number of avoidance tactics to take you away from what it is you think you 'should be doing' that supposedly needs your creative juices to flow.

When I consider the times I am able to write, it is very often free-flowing, and like most artists it seems to come through me rather than from me. I'm just one cog holding the pen or using the keyboard in the bigger system of creation. Often, in exploring and 'getting creative' with clients, it doesn't feel like I am even there at all. We're simply guided in our conversation by questions that come to my mind in what appears to be my own curiosity, yet on reflection it seems it's my curiosity that is being guided.

So, are we creative artists or artists of creation?

It looks to me like we're both. And always both.

When I'm not creating my own story of how I'm not creative, (do you see the irony in that?) I am able to allow the wisdom of a greater creative energy to flow through me. Without my story of 'I am not creative' I have a clearer mind and am able to allow the creative energy of life to flow through me unabated.

That flow does only seem to happen when I am not caught up in that story, caught up in my own little creation of my own reality. In all those times I don't feel creative, I am focused on me and creating a story about myself. It's often a compelling and powerful story.

We talk about writer's block as if it's something that's already there and is for us to overcome. Yet writer's block is just another form of a reality that can only ever be created by the writer. The writer creates writer's block then claims an inability to create.

It seems the times when I don't feel creative are the times when I am personally being my most creative. So creative, in fact, I'm able to create something in my mind that keeps out all other creative forces of nature. Some might say, so creative I'm keeping out God.

Now that IS a powerful creation!

# The Closing of my Casket

This may not be an uplifting chapter, yet I see in writing this, in sharing this, all the while I am not where this describes, I am already uplifted, I am above ground.

I am in the air, I am in the light of day, I am here, I am now, I am love.

So much of what we search for, wait for, supposedly live for, will come at the end of our time. Don't wait to die before you decide to live. Relinquish your quest to preserve that which cannot be retained.

In this I share a darker side so that, maybe, you can see the contrast of the light.

---

I lay in the silk lined box, a soft cushion beneath my back

A tragic kiss of fabric against the sides of my face

My cool hands resting across my still and silent chest.

Drowned in infinite comfort sought so often during life.

I never allowed myself to know it would come, instead

I searched and craved the peace that embraces me now dead.

Oh, to feel just one more time. Something. Some thing. An itch, a dull pain.

The burning cold of oft hated freezing rain

Never to hit my face again.

So much weather of life missed whilst I hunted down

The unity that the inevitable ending of the separate me would bring.

As the lid is placed, the arrival of sombre darkness brings infinite sleep.

No more will the sun be the beacon that I battle

At the start of each precious unappreciated day.

I no longer need to wish I could stay in bed,

All of the world is now the crib I'm impotent to leave.

A hammer strikes its final pound, ringing, one more drives the last nail,

It's over now. I'm in the goneness forever, to be seen no more.

My practice of hiding from life brought to its final bear

None can seek or ridicule me here.

The ultimately victory for the fear of being seen.

A shirt too tight, teeth not quite white, irrelevant and lost in the absence of light.

The thud of the ground beneath and the slowly fading sound

A blanket of thrown earth condemn me, cover me, hide me

In the finalness of rehabilitation with from where I came.

So often I winced at egg on my face whilst oblivious to the soil thrown on me now.

What was afraid to be seen rests away forever unobserved, never shared.

Come, I dream, let me make one more mistake, a finale, let me feel one more drop of rain.

Only now comes the closing truth of 'it's too late,'

Untrodden paths exist no more, ever blind, nothing left to explore.

All that remains will be remains.

I return to be part of the earth, the love of the earth

And seep into the ground.

# Fighting My Addiction

There is no mystery
Everything is clear to see
There is no losing you
My dear friend take me away with you

Nights drawing longer
Times spent in hunger
Temptations running through my mind
Taking over who am I to find

Urges creeping growing screaming
Places voices times and feelings
Never to escape the freedom of you
Summers winters blend in view

When will you return
You're always with me when you leave
The same place within me fights for you
The same place is here just for you

Aching 'til you're here again
Thinking you back when you are gone

Drunk with joy from having you
Drunk with pain from missing you.

# Denying Now

Each time I deny myself the opportunity to love what I am doing right now, I deny myself the opportunity to experience being alive. Whenever I 'would rather be someplace else' or 'would rather be doing something else' I take my consciousness away from the only time and place I have - here and now.

And in that sense, I become unconscious, much like being dead.

Woo hoo! Come on, wake up to now. Do you hear the alarms bells of now ringing?

What is in this moment to remind you that you are alive?

What is in this moment for you to love?

Love is not some idea of the future, to be denied until that future arrives. It's always here for us in every moment, despite how much we might attempt to deny it.

What might it be like to be in love, with this moment, now?

# Listening for What You Want

Getting what you want in life ultimately depends upon the extent to which you listen to the voice of your self-image.

I know of no better way of creating change in the world than taking action, and most times when I don't take action it's because I am listening to the voice of my self-image, what that action might mean about me, rather than listening to my heart and allowing myself to be guided by loving wisdom.

Your self-image will often tell you that you can't always have what you want and chastise you for even thinking that you can.

Yet we live in a universe that will support us in all that we need and want if we are willing to listen to it, if we are willing to listen to, and take action under, the wisdom and guidance of our heart.

# Release Your Dream

Allow your heart's dream out into the open so you yourself can see it.

What's the point of a dream if you only experience it when you're asleep?

Let your dreams out. Speak them, with pride, into your world.

Allow your dreams to be directed by your heart, rather than your fears.

Love your dreams, openly, with joy, love them into being.

# My Selfish Fear

The only thing between us and all the clients, success and love that we desire is an obsession with our self.

In almost every conversation I have with clients, there is one emotion that we all use as a means to hold us back from serving others: fear.

Ultimately this fear is one of rejection: if I do this will I be loved and accepted? A Course in Miracles suggests we all have one basic fear; Am I loved, or am I loveable? Do you recognise that?

People who seem to be dancing in success simply do not listen to these fears. They still experience it, but they see no relevance.

We cannot be of service to others whilst we hold back because of our fear of rejection. Yet to sit on our ability to be of service is surely selfish.

A great measure of self-obsession is the extent to which we listen to our fear of rejection.

The more I listen to this fear, the more concerned I am about me and my self-image over being of service and love to others.

Because of our fear of rejection, it's often suggested we need courage to take action, to love or be of service. Yet courage is only a conceptual distraction to counterbalance an egotistic misbelief in the relevance of fear.

Sure, fear is part of the human condition, and we need do nothing with it except simply choose to not listen to it. Only your ego says you need courage.

To love others and be of service, we must be less selfish and relinquish our obsession with ourselves. We must be willing to love.

*No creature that can fart should ever take life too seriously.*

# Crapping in Your Nest

You don't have to crap in your existing nest to build a new one.

Many of us (and by this I mean I've done this!) continue to convince ourselves that we must hate an existing situation and use that as motivation to find or create a new one. This is particularly common with jobs, where we deny ourselves any opportunity to enjoy our current employment, as doing so seems a kind of betrayal to finding our dream next opportunity.

Yet we do not need to sacrifice happiness now in order to be motivated to attain it in the future. Indeed, happiness is only ever available to us in the present moment, irrespective of circumstances, and each moment we sacrifice it we attempt to step outside of the ever-present creative energy of love.

Whenever I coach someone who wants to change jobs or careers, I'm always looking to help them get back in touch with the unconditional love that is within them, since it is from that place that creative energy flows and we are most receptive to miracles.

And as a bonus we're always at our happiest when we're in touch with the love we are within.

If you want a different job, relearn how to love your existing one. Being the best you can be in your current situation will help create a new situation that is best for you.

Unless, of course, you just want to continue to nest in crap...

# The Simplicity of Your Being

Many try to make the world a better place so they can feel better, yet feeling better, allowing love, is what makes the world a better place.

Without you trying to be somebody, without you even trying to be you, the beauty of you shines and illuminates the beauty of the world.

You can't 'do' being.

Your true, unconditioned being is what radiates when you simply allow, without resistance, without reasoning, without conditions.

In the simplicity of your being, the world becomes a more loving place.

# What Becomes of the Broken-Hearted

Your heart will lift you when you let go of the weight of your broken dreams.

What if your heart cannot be broken? What if your heart is an immutable force of love that has no judgment, only acceptance?

If this is true, something else must be going on in those times when we feel 'heartbroken.'

If love is unconditional acceptance, doesn't it make sense that your heart accepts all? The part of us that does not accept is the part of us that judges, since it is only in judgment we consider something unacceptable.

The part of us that feels distraught in those times we describe as 'heartbroken' is the part of us that had dreams and expectations that have not or will not be met, the part of us that had dreamed and imagined our future, and feels pain at the realisation that what we imagined may not be how it turns out.

It's the part of us that has created an image of our self and how our life would be, and then feels we failed in our negotiation of what the universe was to deliver to us. It is our self-image that is 'heartbroken.'

In those times when we feel broken we don't need to be fixed. We just need to allow ourselves to feel love again, to get back in touch with who we really are.

In those times of 'heartbreak' it is actually our heart that can lift us and carry us out of our pain. It is through acceptance, through love, that we can feel healed from pain and begin to dream again.

# Everything Worth Having Comes Easy

I saw a Facebook post yesterday that said "Nothing worth having comes easy."

Yet, in my experience, the things we all want most in life - love, peace, happiness, are actually the easiest to attain, especially once we get out of the way and allow them.

And when we come from love, anything else we desire may come with an often-forgotten ease.

If it doesn't feel easy, you've forgotten something. The ease and creativity of Love.

# You Don't Need to Fill Holes

When you're in love with your wholeness you don't need to fill any holes.

There is no part of you to be fixed, even when you feel broken. No part of you to be replaced or filled, even when you feel a void.

Love is absolute, all-encompassing, and unconditional. There are no circumstances when you are not a being of love.

Love is the life force that is running through you, that is you. It has no holes. It is the whole. The whole of you.

# How Will You Answer the Call for Love?

If we consider all behaviours as either an expression of love or a call for love, for all acts of fear our invitation is always 'How will we answer the call for love?'

I know that I want to respond to that call, not from a place of fear, anxiousness, judgment or anger, but from a place of love in myself. Only love can teach love.

I cannot either teach love or respond with love if I am feeling resistance or making a judgment. If I am to respond to the call for love with love I must first accept this person is coming from fear, rather than resisting it in my judgment of them with some version of 'They shouldn't be doing that.'

There is a simple truth in that if we believed what they believed we would behave as they behave.

Our response may be speaking an unwelcome truth, a simple embrace, or a simple act of loving kindness. It may be one of force to protect humanity, force to protect our children, force to protect ourselves. We may have to leave a relationship, have someone evicted, or use military force against a terrorist organisation.

Don't be fooled into thinking this is just about terrorists or violent criminals. This is also about the driver who cuts you up with a finger sign on the way to the store, the checkout operator hissing as he packs your bags, or the Facebook friend making less-than-complimentary comments about others, or simply providing a written commentary on how crap their life seems to be.

Let us choose our response to the call for love guided by the wisdom of love itself, not by terror or fear.

In all who you meet, will you respond to the call for love with love?

# Fonz's Watermelon

I read somewhere that when someone jumps off a building, if it's high enough, their body disintegrates as it hits the ground in much the same way as if it were a watermelon.

When I took an overdose in my twenties that resulted in one of those very unpleasant trips to the hospital, I wasn't even aware of my thinking around it. I had been prescribed anti-depressant drugs by my doctor, and at the end of an evening out with some friends for a few drinks it seems I had the thought that it was a good idea to take all the pills at once. Staying at my Mother's home because of the state of my marriage at the time, I can hear her voice in my head even now, relaying to my stepdad what the doctor had said - 'Oh no, that's way too many, you need to call an ambulance right now.'

I've been on this planet in this lifetime a few weeks short of forty-eight years. In the inevitable times of reflection about my life I see it has been rich, eventful, challenging, full, and any number of other adjectives to describe lived and alive. I notice a sense of peace about my mortality, I feel I have lived a full life already, and whilst there is much I still want to do and I definitely don't want to be going anywhere just yet, I'm okay knowing that at any time it may be time to leave. I've no immediate conscious desire to hear Elvis sing My Way whilst my body lay behind that curtain, but I do love the song.

Two divorces, numerous other breakups, the ten years of disownment by my father, that attempted suicide, sexual abuse, an incredibly lonely childhood, the crazy abusive marriage, the struggles with weight and feelings of pointlessness. Merging in thoughts with numerous holidays around the world, scuba diving in the red sea, the joy of fatherhood and crazy, laughter of friendships, six-figure salaries, big houses and fast cars, girlfriends and casual liaisons, intimacy in this profession, road tripping the Californian coast, and the delight of being in my dear Tsilivi.

Full thoughts of a very full life, one that cannot accurately be represented in a few words or paragraphs. And what does it matter, anyways?

I catch myself wondering if I should go buy a watermelon to throw off my balcony, just to see what that looks like.

I can rationalise these thoughts - I couldn't put my eighty-year-old mother through that, or my brother and sisters, and of course, no way would I do that to my son. Cue the discussion in my head of what is fair and what is not...

I've never been suicidal. There have been times when I thought I was. And that is the point.

I thought I was that thought.

Whilst standing on my balcony and noticing my judgment of a mother chastising her child, as they walk past below, a train of memories of my own father blasting into us children and threatening us, passes through my mind. That big old heavy freight train of judgmental thoughts rattles along the tracks.

Unlike the confused very young man, now I can see the judgments without believing I am the judge.

We should have voted to remain. My father should have come with us to the beach instead of reading in the car. The staff should be friendlier with their regulars. She shouldn't wear that until she's lost a few pounds.

They shouldn't have exploded that bomb. He shouldn't jump off that building. Or maybe he should.

I've never been suicidal and I've never been sad. I've just believed in those moments that I am those thoughts, unable in those moments to see I am merely the thinker. And in the brief moments when I am acutely awake, I can even see I am not the thinker either.

All momentarily in a moment to moment life.

Only in those times when I have identified with the content of my thoughts have I sought to take action to manifest those thoughts into that identity.

As a child, I'm sure I dressed up as some superhero. Looking back I at least like to think I did, even though I have no memory of such. And when I imagined that I was Superman, or more likely the Fonz, I thought what I thought they would think.

Until I didn't. Until the thoughts left. Until the brief moment when I was the Fonz had gone. And the guy who imagined his body hitting the ground is the same guy admiring the soaring flight of a dove in the sky.

I am never my thoughts. Even the thought that says I am. It's not necessary to leave this life to be free of our thoughts about it.

Freedom is already here, in that we are already free from our thoughts because our thoughts are not us. We're free even when we imagine we are imprisoned and need to escape.

Twenty years later, I see very clearly that it doesn't really matter what I think, unless I choose that it does. And even then, only I can make that choice matter.

I still care deeply what others think of me, yet I have chosen not to care so much about the fact that I care what others think of me.

I'm the one who gets to choose whether to observe my thoughts as if they are some documentary describing a conspiracy of how the world is and how it should be, or watch them as if they are simply an amusing sitcom almost too outlandish to be real.

And of course, they never are real, and very rarely true. And those thoughts are definitely not me, however loudly they proclaim to be.

Maybe I'll buy some peaches instead.

*Without fear, love is inevitable.*

# Recommended Reading

Dying to be Me by Anita Moorjani

Loveability by Robert Holden

Reinventing Yourself by Steve Chandler

Loving What Is by Byron Katie

Somebody Should Have Told Us! by Jack Pransky

The Inside-Out Revolution by Michael Neill

F**k It by John C. Parkin

A Course in Miracles by Dr. Helen Schucman

Tuesdays with Morrie by Mitch Albom

# About the Author

Phil Goddard is an internationally renowned coach, author, speaker, leadership trainer, and lover of life and humanity. He is a published author and the host of The Coaching Life Podcast. His work centres around transforming relationships through a deeper understanding of love and the nature of how our experience of life is created.

With humour and sincerity, he combines over twenty-one years in I.T. and Telecoms corporate leadership with twelve years as a professional coach, to help organisations build harmonious teams utilising the most potent force in leadership - love. He also works with individuals to help them develop a deeply grounded understanding of the principles behind our human experience and live wonderfully productive, happy lives, connected to love, ease and compassion for humanity.

He has coached Hollywood actors, international models, journalists, artists, authors, film directors, corporate executives, and numerous business owners, leaders and entrepreneurs..

He is also author of *More Musings on Love* and the host of The Coaching Life Podcast (www.coachinglife.show) and challenges his work on happiness by following a few English sports teams.

Phil can be contacted via philg.com and followed on Facebook at fbphil.com

He can often be found on the Greek Island of Zakynthos.

28345727R00109

Printed in Great Britain
by Amazon